STAND 22

£7

STROOD
TO
PADDOCK
WOOD

Vic Mitchell and Keith Smith

MP _Middleton Press_

First published March 1993

ISBN 1 873793 12 X

© Middleton Press 1993

Design - Deborah Goodridge

Published by Middleton Press
    Easebourne Lane
    Midhurst
    West Sussex
    GU29 9AZ
    Tel: (0730) 813169

Printed & bound by Biddles Ltd,
    Guildford and Kings Lynn

INDEX

MAPS

ACKNOWLEDGEMENTS

We are extremely grateful to many of the photographers for assistance so freely given and also to R.M.Casserley, Dr. E.Course, G.Croughton, J.B.Horne, P.Horne, H.N.James, N.Langridge, A.Ll.Lambert, D.Lovett, A.Neale, R.Randell, Mr.D & Dr.S Salter, N.Stanyon and our ever meticulous wives.

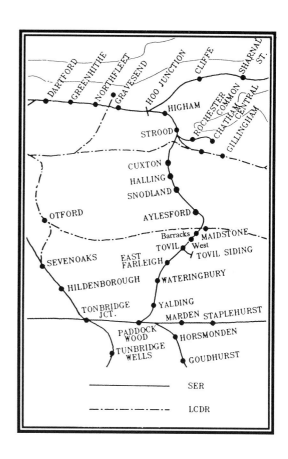

* All maps are to the scale of 25" to 1 mile except those marked * which have been reduced to 20" to 1 mile to incorporate them within page limits.

GEOGRAPHICAL SETTING

The route passes up the Medway Gap in the North Downs, following the River Medway closely as far as Yalding. The chalk of the North Downs has been of economic importance, having been used in paper, lime and cement manufacture in the valley. Lower Greensand features south of Aylesford where the line enters the great fruit growing area of the Garden of England.

It passes through a gap in the Lower Greensand in the Maidstone area and south of Yalding, runs over Brickearth and Wealden Clay on its way to Paddock Wood.

The route is gently graded, climbing only 40ft in its 21 mile length.

```
2nd • SINGLE SINGLE • 2nd
           New Hythe to
New Hythe                    New Hythe
Maidstone West               Maidstone West
        MAIDSTONE WEST
(S)        1/9  Fare  1/9        (S)
For conditions see over  For conditions see over
```
216250

HISTORICAL BACKGROUND

The first line to Maidstone was a single track branch from the South Eastern Railway's 1842 London to Ashford main line at Paddock Wood. This opened on 24th September 1844 and was doubled in 1846.

The SER opened a further route to the county town on 18th June 1856. This was from Strood, which had been a terminus of the North Kent line from London since 10th February 1845. The SER's monopoly of Maidstone's traffic ceased on 1st June 1874, when the London, Chatham & Dover Railway arrived from the west. Their services were extended to Ashford on 1st July 1884.

The SER and LCDR were operated by a managing committee as the South Eastern & Chatham Railway from 1st January 1899. This became part of the Southern Railway in 1923 and British Railways in 1948.

The route was electrified in two stages - north of Maidstone West on 2nd July 1939 and southwards on 12th June 1961.

All stations on the route opened with that part of the line, unless otherwise stated.

PASSENGER SERVICES

The table below gives an indication of the train frequency but excludes services running less than four days per week.

	Strood to Maidstone		Maidstone to Paddock Wood	
	Weekdays	Sundays	Weekdays	Sundays
1844	-	-	6	3
1870	6	5	7	2
1890	8	5	9	2
1906	16	8	10	5
1914	16	9	12	6
1924	19	7	12	3
1934	28	17	15	6
1941	a*	b*	14	5
1954	a*	a*	14	7
1964	a*	a	b†	b
1974	a†	a	b†	b
1983	a†	b	b	b
1993	a	b	b	b

a Two per hour - electric
b One per hour - electric
* One each hour to and from Charing Cross
† Peak hours to and from Charing Cross

In the steam era some trains worked a circular route out from London via Maidstone but the railway managers were reluctant to announce such through train facilities. More recently, in May 1984, managers withdrew through working to London altogether, when the remaining few peak hour trains north of Maidstone ceased to run.

Apart from a few trains in the 1930s, most have stopped at all stations.

1 — Week Days

Dist. M.C.	STATIONS	1 Roundabout. GOODS. A.M. arr.	dep.	2 1 2 & Parl A.M. arr.	dep.	3° 1 2 Class. A.M. arr.	dep.	4 1 2 Class. A.M. arr.	dep.	5 Roundabout. 1 2 Class. P.M. arr.	dep.	6 Roundabout. 1 2 Class. P.M. arr.	dep.	7 GOODS. P.M. arr.	dep.	8 1 2 3 Class. P.M. arr.	dep.
..	Paddock Wood	..	5 35 5 55	..	8 15	..	9 45	..	10 50	1 35	2 0	3 15	4 10	..	4 17	6 15	6 18
3 32	Yalding	6 5	6 15	8 21	8 22	9 51	9 52	10 56	10 57	2 6	2 7	4 16	4 17	4 25	4 45	6 24	6 25
5 13	Wateringbury	6 21	6 31	8 27	8 28	9 57	9 58	11 2	11 3	2 10	2 11	4 22	4 23	4 51	5 6	6 30	6 31
8 11	East Farleigh	6 40	6 45	8 34	8 35	..	..	11 9	11 10	2 16	2 17	4 29	4 30	5 14	5 20	6 38	6 39
..	Ticket Platform			8 40	8 43	10 6	10 8	11 16	11 18	2 22	2 24	4 35	4 38			6 43	6 44
9 79	Maidstone	6 50	7 30	8 45		10 10		11 20		2 26	2 50	4 40	5 0	5 40		6 45	

Week Days — continued. / Sundays.

Dist. M.C.	STATIONS	9 GOODS P.M. arr.	dep.	10 GOODS P.M. arr.	dep.	11 Roundabout 1 2 3 Class. P.M. arr.	dep.	1 1 2 3 Class A.M. arr.	dep.	2 1 2 3 Class. P.M. arr.	dep.
..	Paddock Wood	6 35	7 0	9	5	7 25	8 45	..	9 23	..	8 40
3 22	Yalding	7 10	7 15	9	13	8 51	8 52	9 29	9 30	8 46	8 47
5 13	Wateringbury	7 21	7 31	9	18	8 57	8 58	9 35	9 36	8 52	8 53
8 11	East Farleigh	7 40	7 44	9	25	9 5	9 6	9 42	9 43	8 59	9 0
..	Ticket Platform	..	..	..	..	9 11	9 13	9 47	9 49	9 5	9 7
9 79	Maidstone	7 50		9 30	9 50	9 15	9 40	9 50		9 10	

No. 3 Train is Third Class for Passengers booked through from Stations on Ramsgate and Ashford and Hastings Branches.
All Down Trains from Paddock Wood must approach and enter Maidstone Station with great caution.
Special Trains (Passenger, Goods, or Ballast), not stopping at Maidstone, must run through that Station at a speed not exceeding 10 miles per hour; but no Train will run through Maidstone without special instructions to do so.

SPECIAL GOODS and COAL TRAINS run as required between Strood and Tunbridge. These Trains to be telegraphed from Strood to all Stations.

Tickets of all Down Trains examined at Paddock Wood. May 1870

TONBRIDGE JUNCTION, PADDOCK WOOD, and MAIDSTONE WEST.—South Eastern and Chatham.

July 1914

TONBRIDGE, PADDOCK WOOD, HAWKHURST, and MAIDSTONE WEST.

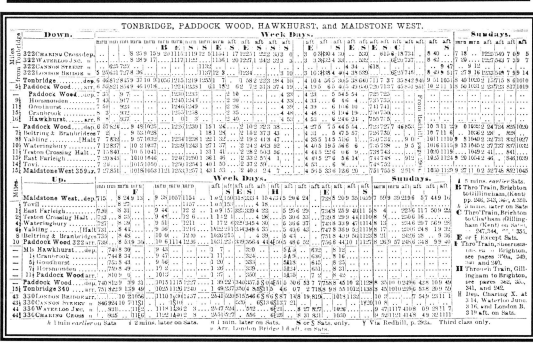

August 1934

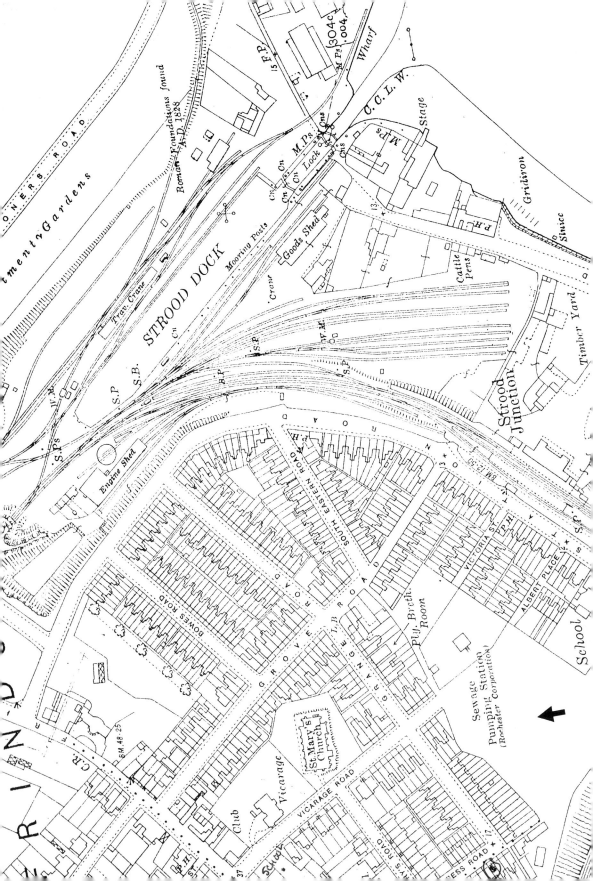

STROOD

I.   The 1934 survey shows the line from Gravesend emerging from Higham Tunnel on the left. Until 1856 trains ran into a terminus situated where the cattle pens are shown. Lower centre is the former LCDR route from London, opened by the East Kent Railway on 29th March 1858. This continued across the centre of the three Rochester Bridges, part of the trackbed being marked *Viaduct*. Nearby are two short sidings which had formed a link between the SER and LCDR, this being in use from 1856 until 1860 and between 1877 and 1891. The left bridge came into use on 20th July 1891 when the SER's branch to Rochester Common opened. It was extended to Chatham Central and closed on 1st October 1911. The complex story of the railway crossings over the Medway will be told in a future album, along with details of the LCDR's Rochester Bridge station. Aveling & Porter's Invicta Works is lower right, this being noted for the production of steam rollers and geared railway engines of the type seen in picture no. 26.

1.   The terminal station was named "Rochester" until 1849 and "Strood, Rochester and Chatham" until 1852. The station shown was "Strood Junction" for much of its life. This is the northward view on 28th March 1914. (D.Cullum coll.)

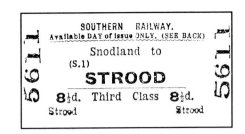

SOUTHERN   RAILWAY.
Available DAY of issue ONLY. (SEE BACK)
Snodland   to
(S.1)
STROOD
8½d. Third Class 8½d.
Strood   Strood

T1965

5611

2.   Taken on the same day, this picture shows the southern approaches, with the ex-LCDR high level line and the curve to Rochester on the left. The straight line is the route that we will follow to Maidstone. Note the carriage sidings, centre. (D.Cullum coll.)

3.   Seen in April 1933, this wagon hoist was situated south of the signal box shown in the last picture, the latter being largely obscured by a bush in this one. Both are marked on the map. Wagons ran under gravity down the line on the right into the mills and ran back downhill into the hoist, which restored them to yard level. (L.Catchpole)

4. Signalled for the Chatham line in this 1936 record is class R no.1659, propelling a push-pull set. The controls were pneumatically operated, hence the large number of hoses on the buffer beam. (P.Ransome Wallis/National Railway Museum)

5. The up starting signals are on the right, the ones in the distance being those featured in the previous photograph. The ringed arms gave access to the awkwardly shaped goods yard laid out around the dock, which had once formed the entrance to the Thames & Medway Canal to Gravesend - see Kent & East Sussex Waterways (Middleton Press). (H.C.Casserley)

6. Taken on the same day as the previous picture (28th May 1938), R class 0-4-4T no.1669 waits to depart south. The timetable for the train was Gillingham depart 3.58pm, reverse at Strood at 4.14pm, call at Maidstone West, Paddock Wood, Tonbridge, Tunbridge Wells West, Crowborough, Uckfield and then all stations to Brighton, arriving at 6.42pm. There was a similar train leaving Strood at 8.55am. (H.C.Casserley)

7. An up freight on 6th June 1959 takes the direct connection to the North Kent line, relaid in 1939. Also undertaken at this time was the demolition of the signal box. Its replacement is on the left, having been built on the site of two curved sidings. The two sidings left of centre were electrified for stabling stock. The locomotive is class Q1 from 1942. (J.J.Smith)

8. The SER was noted for poor passenger waiting accommodation, cheap wooden buildings being widely used. Seen in 1966, this one had been planned for replacement in 1939, but World War II intervened. In 1973 it was superseded by an even cheaper style of building, known as CLASP and devoid even of a pitched roof. (J.N.Faulkner)

9. On 13th May 1971 the 16.58 Maidstone West to Charing Cross service is passing under the former LCDR main line, the bridge span of which had been replaced in 1927. Note that only one of the two up sidings remained. General goods traffic ceased on 16th August 1971 but coal and china clay traffic continued. (M.J.Furnell)

SOUTH OF STROOD

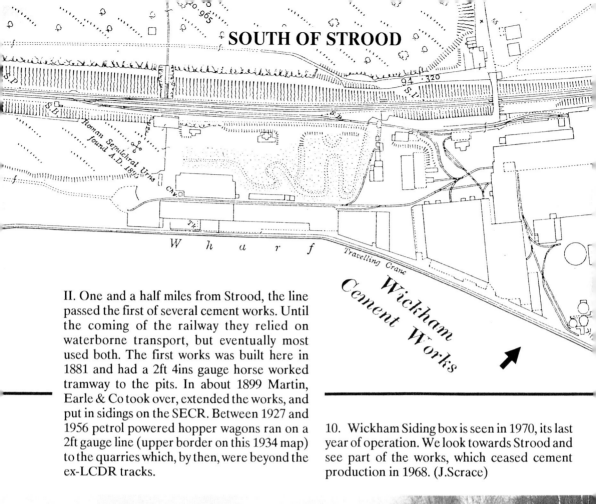

Wickham Cement Works

Travelling Crane

II. One and a half miles from Strood, the line passed the first of several cement works. Until the coming of the railway they relied on waterborne transport, but eventually most used both. The first works was built here in 1881 and had a 2ft 4ins gauge horse worked tramway to the pits. In about 1899 Martin, Earle & Co took over, extended the works, and put in sidings on the SECR. Between 1927 and 1956 petrol powered hopper wagons ran on a 2ft gauge line (upper border on this 1934 map) to the quarries which, by then, were beyond the ex-LCDR tracks.

10. Wickham Siding box is seen in 1970, its last year of operation. We look towards Strood and see part of the works, which ceased cement production in 1968. (J.Scrace)

CUXTON

11.   While the SER was noted for its mean timber and boarded stations in the 1840s, in 1858 it provided the new line to Maidstone with buildings to the opposite extreme. Tiny Cuxton was graced with this magnificent structure. In contrast the down signal arm appears to have rotted at its lower edge.
(Lens of Sutton)

12.   A typical pre-electrification train departs from the down platform. Class D no.1075 is coupled to a Birdcage set, so called because of the guard's look-out on the roof at each end of three coaches. The locomotive was built by Dubs & Co in 1903 and lasted until 1956.
(D.Cullum coll.)

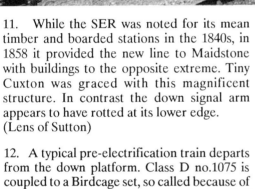

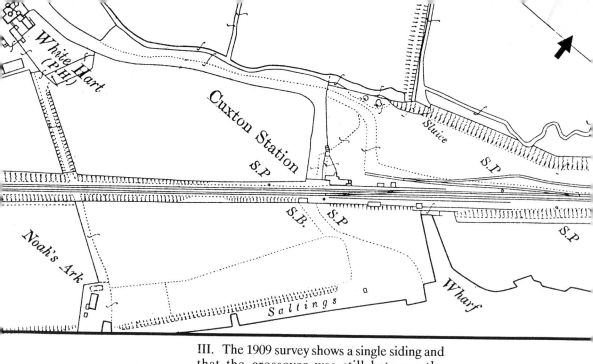

III. The 1909 survey shows a single siding and that the crossover was still between the platforms.

13. The River Medway is visible on the left; Weekes Halling Cement Works is in the distance and the minimal goods yard appears on the right. This closed on 5th June 1961. In 1988 a siding was laid for Lowfield Distribution but no traffic was handled there. (D.Cullum coll.)

14.   This is the intending passenger's perspective in 1960. The position of the steps is revealed on the maps. A ticket office on the down platform would be most unexpected at this quiet location. (Lens of Sutton)

IV.   By the time of the 1932 edition the crossover had been moved to a site close to the industrial siding.

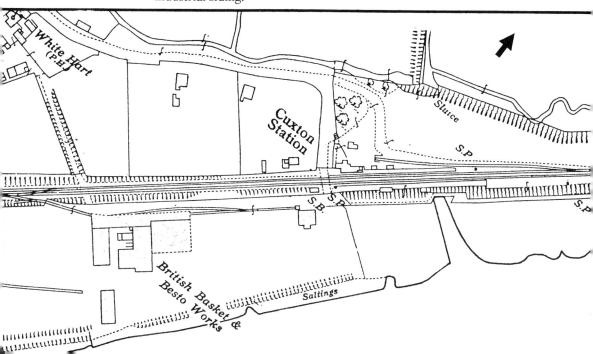

15.   *Right of Way Act 1932. The British Transport Commission hereby give Notice that this Roadway is not Dedicated to the Public.* So reads the notice on the hand worked gates in 1970. They were unlocked from the signal box. The box and gates were all in use 23 years later. (J.Scrace)

16.   No.73142 approaches Cuxton on 14th April 1987 with a Chartex round tour from Victoria via Dover, Strood and Maidstone West, which used the Venice Simplon Orient Express coaches. The bridge in the distance is for the M2 motorway. On the left are the points of the up electrified loop . (J.Scrace)

17. When recorded in 1988 the down side shelter retained its intricate valance, while the up building still displayed its coupled chimneys and finely patterned cast iron windows. By 1992 they were all boarded up. (J.Scrace)

18. Formerly known as "weed killing", this *weed control* train is running north on 16th May 1989, with no.20901 heading and no.20904 at the rear. The footbridge was added at the time of electrification. (S.C.Nash)

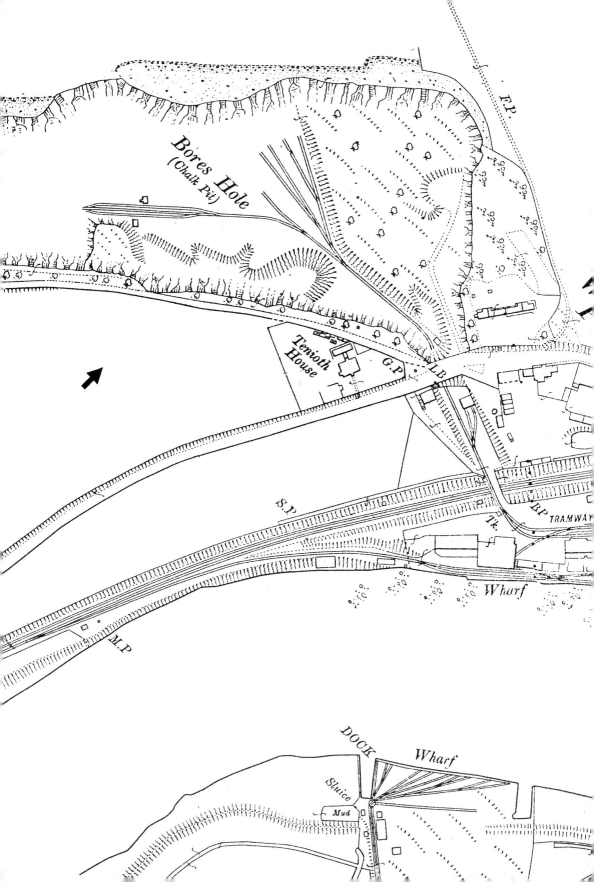

Bores Hole
(Chalk Pit)

F.P

Tenioth
House

G.P

L.B

S.P

T.k

B.P TRAMWAY

Wharf

M.P

DOCK

Wharf

Sluice

Mud

SOUTH OF CUXTON

19. Sadly, by 1992 this was the only cement works in the Medway Valley to be rail connected, but no cement was sent by train at that time. The works is north of Halling and west of the line but the sidings are to the east of it. The chalk slopes of the North Downs are in the background as a 4CEP or class 411 unit speeds by on 16th May 1992. (V.Mitchell)

V. Weekes Halling Works became part of British Portland Cement in 1910, the year after this map was published. The tramway was 4ft 3½ins gauge and was steam worked. The company had a Manning Wardle 0-6-0ST *(Monica)* to work its standard gauge sidings which were removed in 1935, the works having closed in 1921.

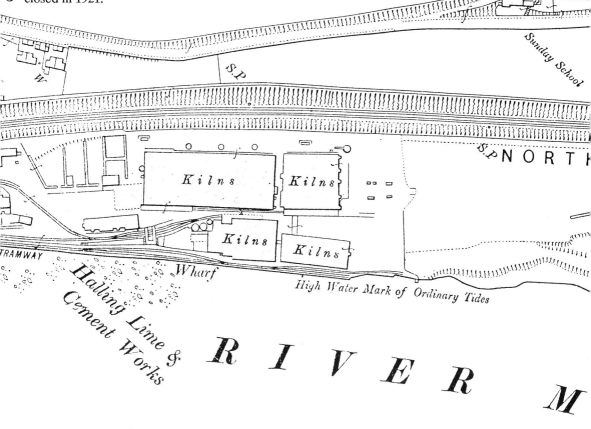

HALLING

20.   The architecture here differs from the imposing style seen elsewhere on the route. This is due to the fact that this station was a latecomer, not opening until 1st March 1890.

21.   The down train comprises two push-pull sets, with the locomotive sandwiched in the middle, the fireman being its sole occupant. The gate on the right is on the siding to Halling Manor Cement Works - see the map after next (no. VII). (D.Cullum coll.)

The bridge at the end of the platforms carries the Rochester Road, now A228. The footbridge dates from 1894. (Lens of Sutton)

22. To the left of the building are gates which gave access to an end loading dock and two sidings. The bracket supporting the loading gauge is also visible. The goods yard closed on 4th September 1961. (Lens of Sutton)

23. A northward view includes the station master's office (left) and the signal box which remained in use until 6th February 1972. Staff crossings were normally whitewashed at the edges only. (Lens of Sutton)

24.   By 16th April 1982, the 14.05 Hoo
Junction to Tonbridge freight service had
degenerated to two wagons, no challenge for
no.33058. Viewed from Cemetery Road
bridge, Rochester Road bridge largely
obscures the platforms. (J.S.Petley)

25.   With a disused chalk quarry in the
background, no.33042 departs with the 11.10
Halling to Greenford cement train on 11th July
1988. By then the platform canopies had gone
and the down platform shelter had been
replaced. This has subsequently been
superseded by a glazed model. Southampton
(Northam) was another destination for cement
at this time but all the sidings were mothballed
in the 1990s due to the recession. (J.Scrace)

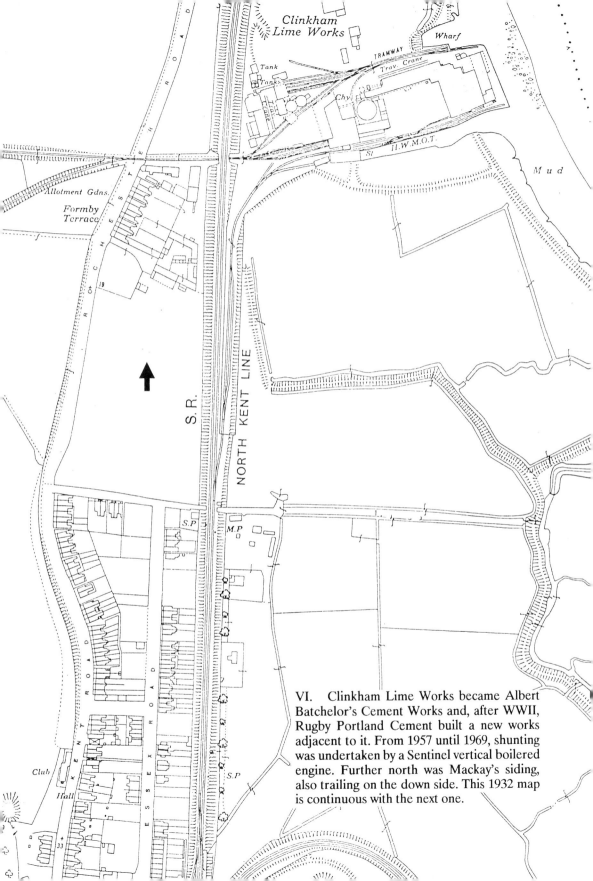

Clinkham
Lime Works

Wharf

TRAMWAY

Trav. Crane

Tank

Tanks

Chy.

H.W.M.O.T.

St.

Mud

Allotment Gdns.

Formby
Terrace

19

ROCHESTER ROAD

S.R.

NORTH KENT LINE

S.P.

M.P.

S.P.

Club

Hall

KENT ROAD

ESSEX ROAD

33

S.P.

VI.   Clinkham Lime Works became Albert
Batchelor's Cement Works and, after WWII,
Rugby Portland Cement built a new works
adjacent to it. From 1957 until 1969, shunting
was undertaken by a Sentinel vertical boilered
engine. Further north was Mackay's siding,
also trailing on the down side. This 1932 map
is continuous with the next one.

Halling Fresh

G.P

L.B

nd

Station

Skeleton
found
A.D. 1912

Sewage Works
(Strood R.D. Council)

S.B.

S.P

S.Ps

Marsh Road

VII. Halling Station is at the top of this map
and Halling church is below centre,
surrounded by Halling Manor Cement Works.
This had been established as a lime works in
1873 and commenced cement production in
1878. From 1893 it was operated by Hilton,
Anderson, Brooks & Co and became part of
APC in 1900, closing in about 1920. The
quarry linc was latterly standard gauge and
steam worked. Note that it had a level crossing
over the Rochester Road.

S.P

DOCK

CEMETERY

S.P

Bathing
Pond

CEMETERY ROAD

Inst.

P.O.

Allotment Gardens

Wharf

FERRY

Five Bells
(P.H.)

Bishop's
Palace
G. Y. (Rems. of)

ROAD

Chapel
(Rems. of)

St. John the
Baptist's Ch.
(Vic.)

Ferry

Halling Manor
Cement Works
(Disused)

P.H.

Mud Wharf

Stone

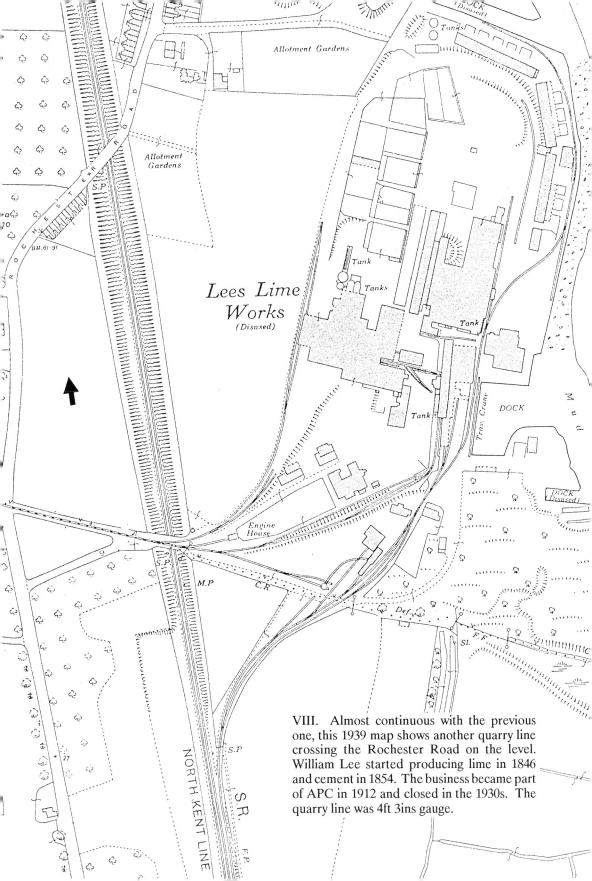

Allotment Gardens

Allotment
Gardens

S.P

BM.61·91

ROCHESTER ROAD

Lees Lime
Works
(Disused)

Tank

Tanks

Tank

Tank

DOCK (Disused)

Tanks

Trav. Crane

DOCK

Mud

DOCK
(Disused)

Engine
House

S.P

M.P

C.R.

Def.

Sl.

F.P.

27

S.P

NORTH KENT LINE

S.R.

F.P.

VIII. Almost continuous with the previous
one, this 1939 map shows another quarry line
crossing the Rochester Road on the level.
William Lee started producing lime in 1846
and cement in 1854. The business became part
of APC in 1912 and closed in the 1930s. The
quarry line was 4ft 3ins gauge.

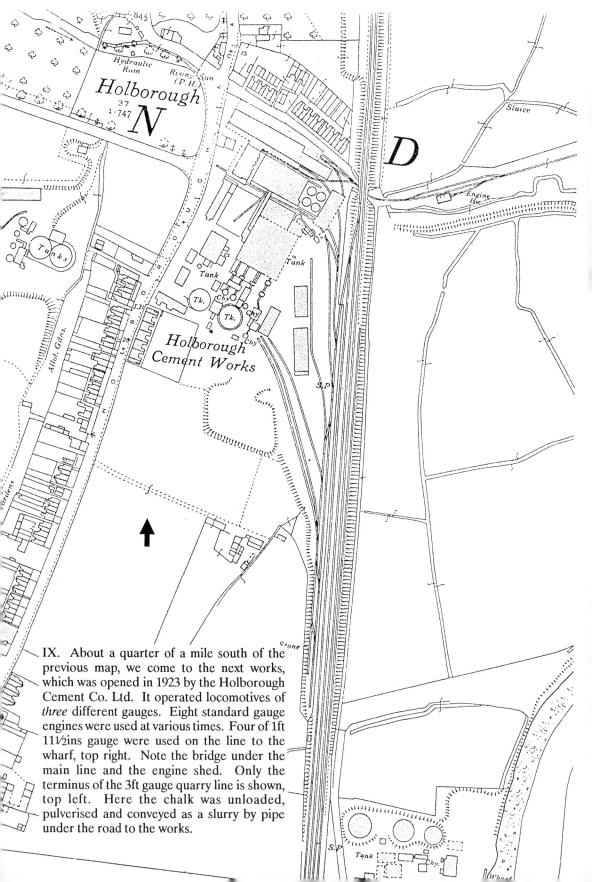

Holborough
37
1·747

N

D

Hydraulic
Ram

Rising Sun
(P.H.)

Sluice

Engine
Ho.

Tanks

Tank

Tank

Tk.

Chy

Chy

Tk.

Chy

Allot. Gdns.

Holborough
Cement Works

S.P

Stone

S.P

Tank

Chy

Wharf

IX. About a quarter of a mile south of the previous map, we come to the next works, which was opened in 1923 by the Holborough Cement Co. Ltd. It operated locomotives of *three* different gauges. Eight standard gauge engines were used at various times. Four of 1ft 11½ins gauge were used on the line to the wharf, top right. Note the bridge under the main line and the engine shed. Only the terminus of the 3ft gauge quarry line is shown, top left. Here the chalk was unloaded, pulverised and conveyed as a slurry by pipe under the road to the works.

CEMENT WORKS LOCOMOTIVES

26. Aveling & Porter geared locomotives were used widely in the cement works of Kent. This 1926 model had 6ft diameter driving wheels and was moved to the Bluebell Railway in 1964. This and the next picture were taken at APCM's Holborough Works on 9th August 1952. (H.C.Casserley)

27. *Felspar* was built by Manning Wardle in 1914 with 3ft driving wheels and arrived at the works in 1937. Cement manufacture requires large quantities of gypsum, this being conveyed by rail from the only source in the South of England at Mountfield, north of Hastings. (H.C.Casserley)

28. Seen at the Holborough Works on 22nd May 1971 are two 1928 Pecketts, *Longfield* and *Hornpipe*. *Longfield* (left) had come from

Greenhithe in 1960 but *Hornpipe* had been supplied new and was moved to Quainton Road in 1972 for preservation. (J.Scrace)

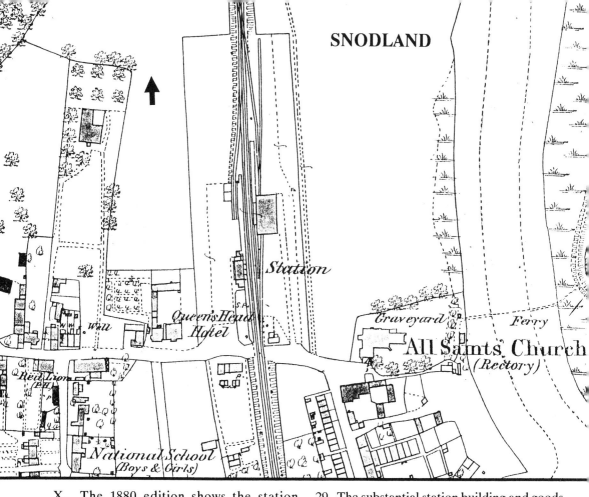

SNODLAND

X. The 1880 edition shows the station surrounded by fields despite the population having trebled from about 1000 during the previous twenty years.

29. The substantial station building and goods shed were completed in 1858, the latter having a fenestrated chimney stack. The 5-ton capacity crane is just in the picture. The locomotive is an ex-LCDR A class 0-4-4T. (Lens of Sutton)

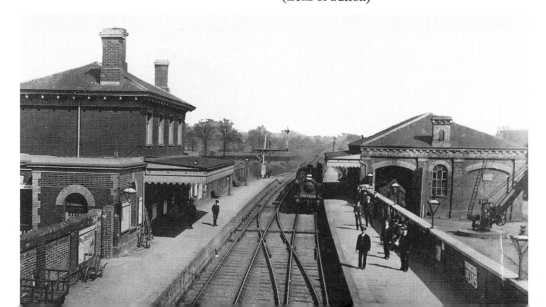

30. The massive chimney of the paper mills dwarfs the church tower. The mill was of importance in relation to rail traffic while the church was of importance on the Pilgrims Way, which crossed the Medway by ferry adjacent to its graveyard. (D.Cullum coll)

XI. The 1909 survey shows additional sidings, these having been laid in 1896. Look for a narrow gauge line between the goods yard and the waterfront. At the lower border is part of Townsend Hook's private siding.

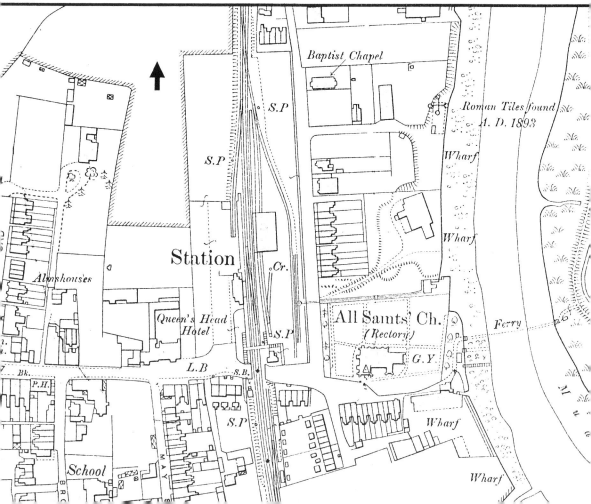

31. A generous shelter was provided on the down platform, the goods shed wall providing most of the structure. The shed once received large quantities of rags for paper making at the Townsend Hook Works. (Lens of Sutton)

32. The west and south elevations are seen in 1967, along with an array of porcelain insulators, then still in use with uninsulated copper wires. The gas works was of no benefit to the railway here, all coal arriving by barge. (J.N.Faulkner)

33. A 1971 view of the typical SER signal box includes an atypical feature - an extension to house the gate wheel. This was presumably added when the separate gatekeeper was eliminated. Lifting barriers replaced the gates on 28th January 1973. (J.Scrace)

34. The goods yard closed on 10th June 1963 and the goods shed was subsequently used commercially. A stove pipe replaced its elegant chimneys and the building was later demolished. (C.Hall)

35. The well preserved station building was recorded in July 1988, along with the 1883 footbridge. The station is now separated from the main part of the village by a busy main road. (J.Scrace)

36. On 7th December 1991 4CEP no.1601 was working the 12.46 Strood to Paddock Wood and had been fitted with a headlight to warn track workers of its approach. Only the goods shed wall remains as evidence of a once busy depot. In 1993 the building was boarded up awaiting a tenant. (P.G.Barnes)

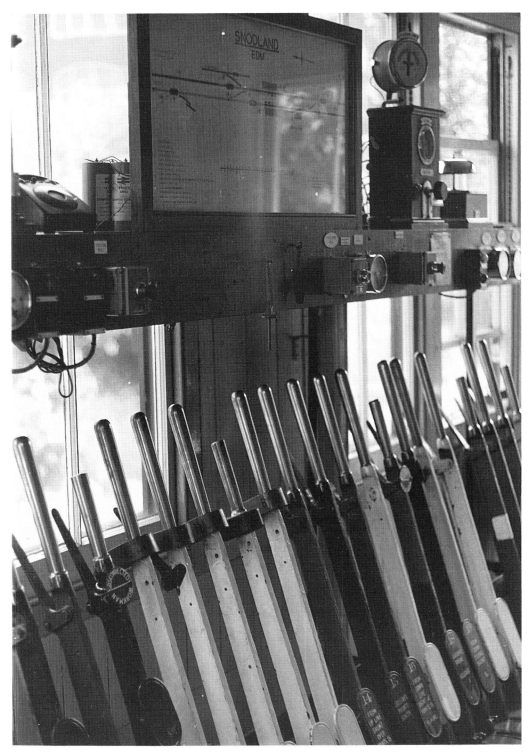

37. Photographed in May 1992, the 26-lever frame was still active, with only eight levers out of use (painted white). A closing switch for Halling was still in place, although the box had gone twenty years earlier. (V.Mitchell)

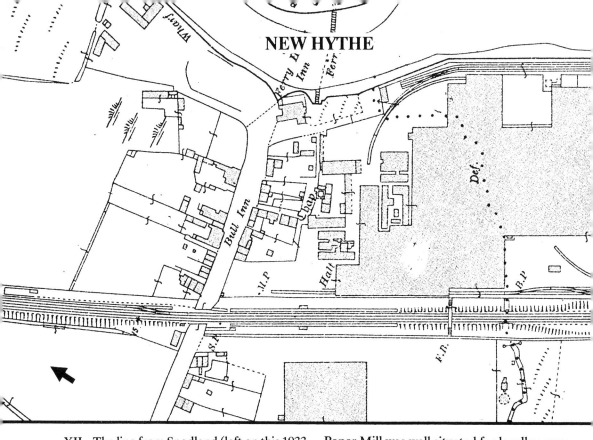

NEW HYTHE

XII. The line from Snodland (left on this 1933 map) passes a short siding which was later extended by the Seaborne Coal Co. Next is a level crossing and New Hythe Halt. Reed's Paper Mill was well situated for locally grown timber and also for chalk, another important constituent of paper.

38. The halt was opened on 9th December 1929 and ceased to be thus designated in July 1939. The platforms were rebuilt and buildings erected at the time of electrification. The up starting signal (left) has Snodland's distant below it. (Lens of Sutton)

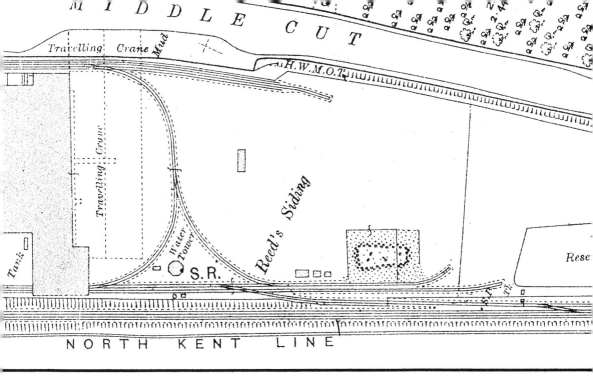

39. U class no.1618 was built at Brighton in 1928 and withdrawn from traffic in 1964. It was the second locomotive to leave the scrapyard at Barry and was at New Hythe from 1969 until 1972, when it was moved to Tenterden. Following successful steaming there, it was transferred to the Bluebell Railway in 1977. (C.Hall)

40.   Pictured in May 1971, the gates were replaced by full barriers on 19th November 1972, these being controlled from the adjacent signal box. In the background is part of the Reed industrial complex which justified the provision of a station here. The box and semaphore signals were still in use in 1993. (J.Scrace)

41.   Reed's water tower dominates the scene as their Ruston diesel shunter waits to take over tankers from the class 33. Fuel oil and coal continued to arrive by rail at the Brookgate up siding in 1993. (C.Hall)

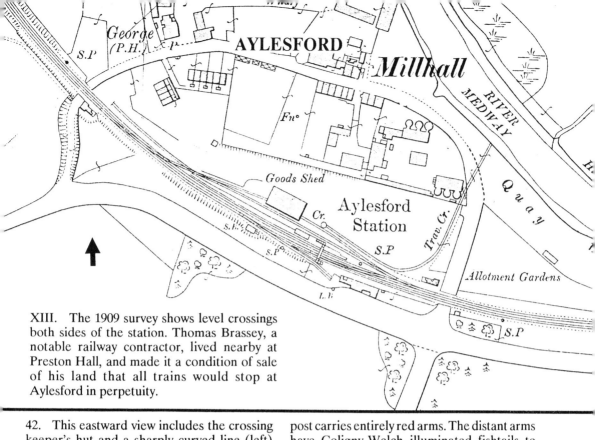

42. This eastward view includes the crossing keeper's hut and a sharply curved line (left) marked on the map as being used by a travelling crane to the quay. The tapered signal post carries entirely red arms. The distant arms have Coligny-Welch illuminated fishtails to distinguish their red and green lights from home signals. (Lens of Sutton)

43. The same scene in the early years of the SR reveals revised signalling and the position of the new signal box. The location of its predecessor is shown on the 1909 map and in the next picture. (Lens of Sutton)

XIV. The 1933 edition includes a petrol depot siding on the right. The curve through the station is on a 28 chain radius.

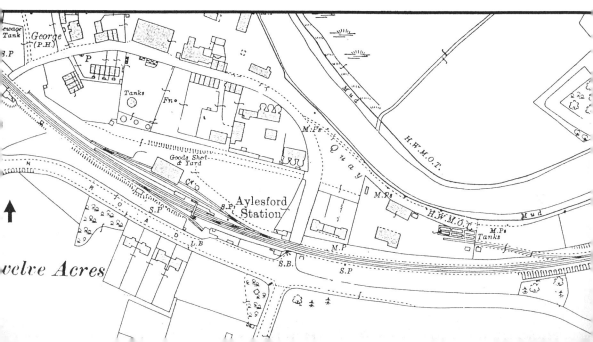

44. Class H 0-4-4T no.1274 passes the former signal box on 20th May 1936. On the right is the lengthy goods dock on the loop west of the goods shed. (H.C.Casserley)

45. As at Snodland, a large goods shed and 5-ton crane were provided, although the local population here was about double at around 2000. It only exceeded 3000 after WWI. The short siding on the right served a loading dock. The shed and signal box (in the distance) were still standing in 1993. (Lens of Sutton)

46. A 1967 photograph includes the disused points that once served a second siding, and the 1888 footbridge. The goods yard closed later than most on the route, on 2nd December 1974. (J.N.Faulkner)

47. Conversely, the crossing was fitted with barriers earlier than most on the line, on 27th September 1964, these being controlled from the adjacent signal box. The house was presumably built for the crossing keeper. The Regent Petrol Depot in the distance was rail served. (J.N.Faulkner)

48.   Pictured in 1971, this architectural masterpiece subsequently received a Grade II listing and in 1988 was the subject of a £250,000 restoration scheme. The Caen stone quoins and Kentish Ragstone infills were repaired, the chimneys replaced, the cast iron windows grit blasted and their 2805 glass diamonds replaced. (J.Scrace)

EAST OF AYLESFORD

49. Half a mile east of the station, this crossing is situated at the south end of the road bridge which crosses the Medway and leads into the historic village. Barriers were installed on 29th November 1965, the box being taken out of use on 8th January 1978 when CCTV was installed. (J.Scrace)

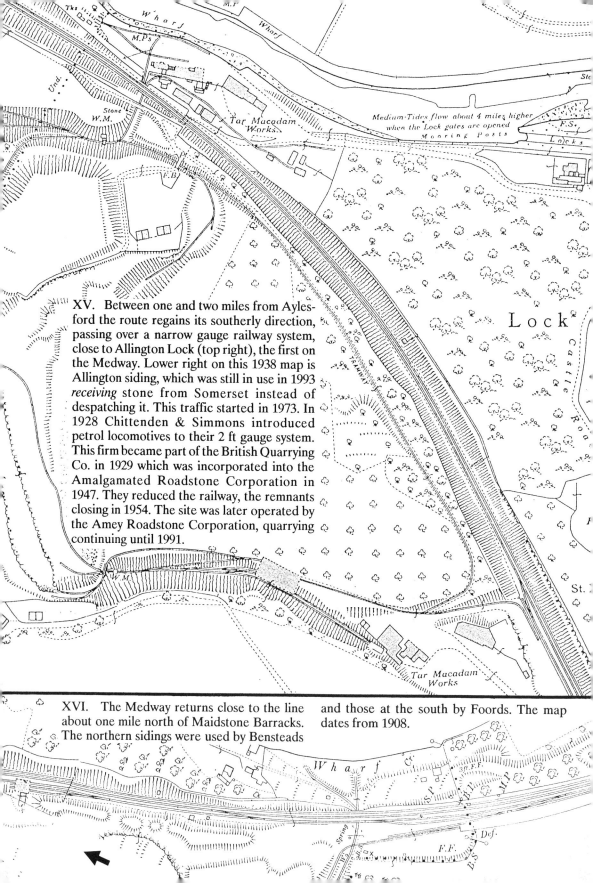

XV. Between one and two miles from Aylesford the route regains its southerly direction, passing over a narrow gauge railway system, close to Allington Lock (top right), the first on the Medway. Lower right on this 1938 map is Allington siding, which was still in use in 1993 *receiving* stone from Somerset instead of despatching it. This traffic started in 1973. In 1928 Chittenden & Simmons introduced petrol locomotives to their 2 ft gauge system. This firm became part of the British Quarrying Co. in 1929 which was incorporated into the Amalgamated Roadstone Corporation in 1947. They reduced the railway, the remnants closing in 1954. The site was later operated by the Amey Roadstone Corporation, quarrying continuing until 1991.

XVI. The Medway returns close to the line about one mile north of Maidstone Barracks. The northern sidings were used by Bensteads and those at the south by Foords. The map dates from 1908.

MAIDSTONE BARRACKS

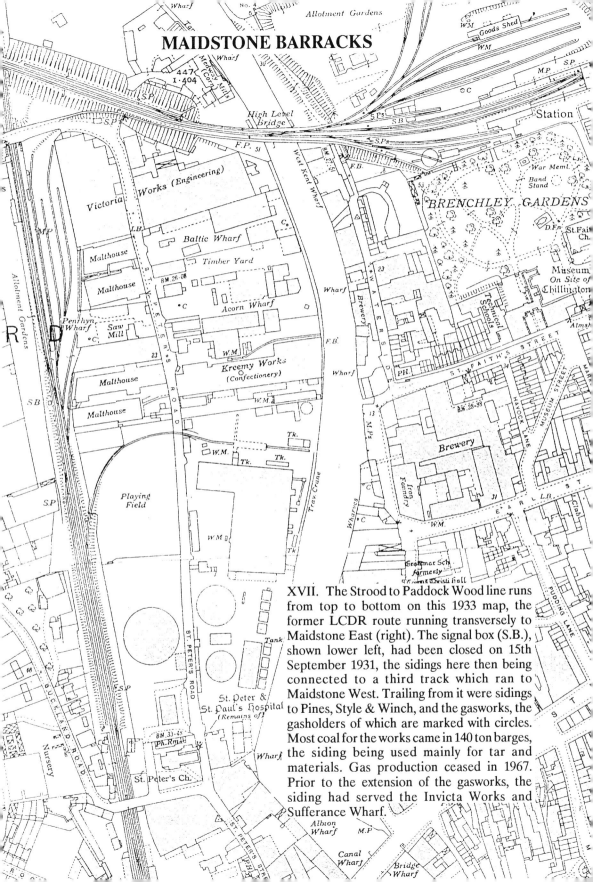

XVII. The Strood to Paddock Wood line runs from top to bottom on this 1933 map, the former LCDR route running transversely to Maidstone East (right). The signal box (S.B.), shown lower left, had been closed on 15th September 1931, the sidings here then being connected to a third track which ran to Maidstone West. Trailing from it were sidings to Pines, Style & Winch, and the gasworks, the gasholders of which are marked with circles. Most coal for the works came in 140 ton barges, the siding being used mainly for tar and materials. Gas production ceased in 1967. Prior to the extension of the gasworks, the siding had served the Invicta Works and Sufferance Wharf.

50.   Four electrified sidings were provided, each accommodating four coaches. The facility became redundant in about 1980, the site later being used by a builders merchant. Note the profusion of malthouses. In the siding is a 2HAL unit, headcoded 84. Down electric trains divided at Strood, the front portion going to Gillingham and the rear to Maidstone West. (Lens of Sutton)

51.   The station was built at a cost of £500 and opened on 1st July 1874 in response to the arrival of the LCDR in the town. That company's bridge was provided with a footway which gave direct access to the town centre. Oil tankers stand in the sidings which were laid down in 1877. (Lens of Sutton)

52. The up side building dates from 1876 and contains waiting, booking and toilet facilities. The steps connect with the road bridge, no separate footbridge being required. The building was demolished in 1991 and replaced by a glazed shelter. (C.Hall)

53. A 2EPB unit arrives from Strood on 11th July 1988 having just passed the site of Maidstone Corporation's siding, which trailed from the down line. Behind the camera, an electrified up siding had been in use in earlier years. A modern shelter has superseded this wooden structure. (J.Scrace)

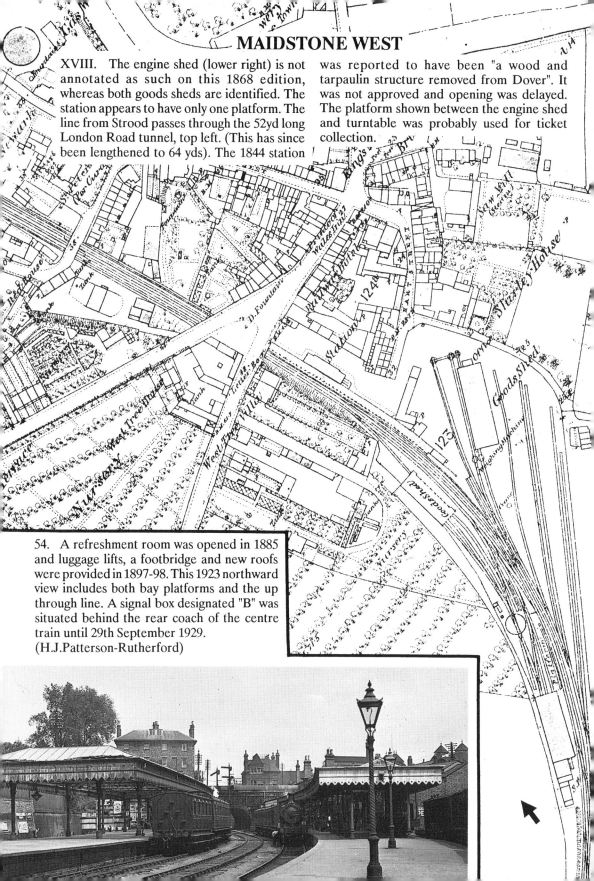

MAIDSTONE WEST

XVIII.   The engine shed (lower right) is not annotated as such on this 1868 edition, whereas both goods sheds are identified. The station appears to have only one platform. The line from Strood passes through the 52yd long London Road tunnel, top left. (This has since been lengthened to 64 yds). The 1844 station was reported to have been "a wood and tarpaulin structure removed from Dover". It was not approved and opening was delayed. The platform shown between the engine shed and turntable was probably used for ticket collection.

54.   A refreshment room was opened in 1885 and luggage lifts, a footbridge and new roofs were provided in 1897-98. This 1923 northward view includes both bay platforms and the up through line. A signal box designated "B" was situated behind the rear coach of the centre train until 29th September 1929.
(H.J.Patterson-Rutherford)

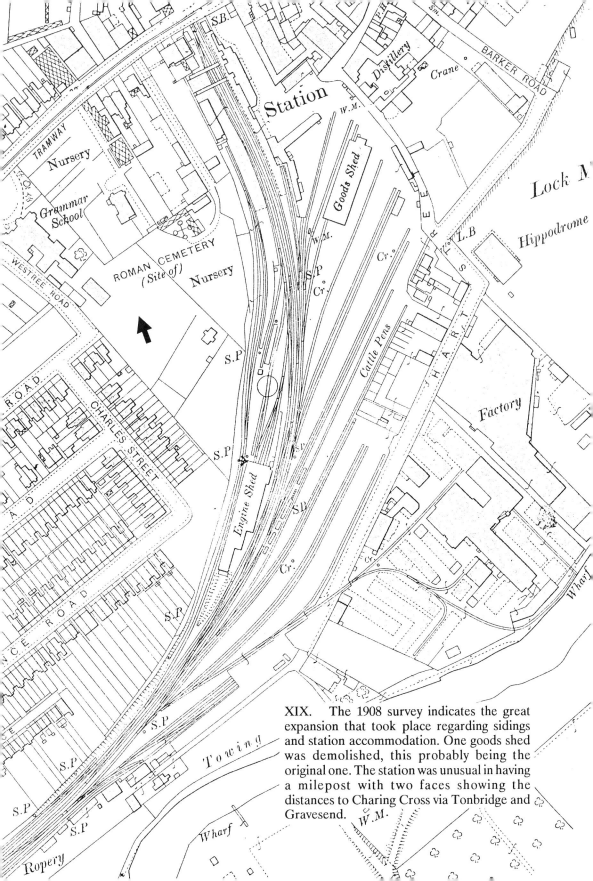

Station

Distillery

Crane

BARKER ROAD

TRAMWAY

Nursery

Grammar School

W.M.

Goods Shed

Lock M

Hippodrome

ROMAN CEMETERY *(Site of)*

Nursery

WESTREE ROAD

W.M.

S.P.

Cr.

Cr.

L.B

S.P.

Cattle Pens

HART

Factory

ROAD

CHARLES STREET

S.P.

Engine Shed

S.P.

S.B.

Cr.

Wharf

S.P.

Cr.

ROAD

S.P.

S.P.

S.P.

Towing

S.P.

Ropery

Wharf

W.M.

XIX.   The 1908 survey indicates the great
expansion that took place regarding sidings
and station accommodation. One goods shed
was demolished, this probably being the
original one. The station was unusual in having
a milepost with two faces showing the
distances to Charing Cross via Tonbridge and
Gravesend.

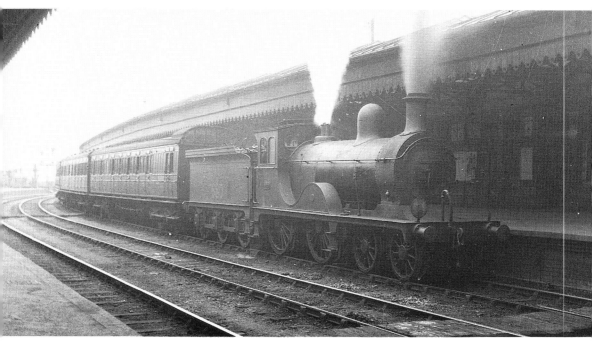

55. No.680 is a class G 4-4-0 and is seen in the up platform on 23rd April 1927 with a Birdcage set. The up and down designations are reversed as the lines pass the signal box south of the platforms. The engine was one of five cancelled from an order of ten by the Great North of Scotland Railway. Designed by Pickersgill, the builder was Neilson, Reid & Co. (H.C.Casserley)

56. The slender based signal box was sited between nos. 8 and 9 sidings, there being 14 in total. An independent third track for goods traffic ran from here to Tovil. Shunting on 3rd December 1932 is no. A337 of class R1, built in 1888 and in use until 1960. (H.C.Casserley)

57.   The three-road locomotive shed was allocated 17 engines at the time of its closure in 1933. This and the next two pictures were taken on 3rd December 1932. Classes represented are F1 (by 1205), C (by A711) and H (by 1310). (H.C.Casserley)

58. This and the previous picture show both vacuum and air brake hoses fitted. This was due to the LCDR and SER having different braking systems. No. A31 is of class F1 and is standing by the typical SER double-wheeled water valve. (H.C.Casserley)

60. Class 01 no. A 373 stands between the coal stack and a heap of ash on 1st October 1932. The empty shed remained unused until demolished in about 1937 but the 45ft turntable was in use until 1939. (H.C.Casserley)

59. No. A31 is waiting on the up main line, while an up train is signalled to depart. The prefix "A" was used by the SR on ex-SECR locomotives until 1931, when it was replaced by "1". (H.C.Casserley)

61.　In contrast to the previous Maidstone pictures taken in poor winter light, here class U1 no.31904 basks in the sun on 26th July 1953. It is running from Gillingham shed to Wateringbury from where it will work a return ramblers special back to London. (N.Sprinks)

63.　The coal stage is right of centre and the water tank is to the right of that. Blowing off near it is class D1 no.31739 at the head of eight coaches forming the 6.36pm to Charing Cross on Easter Monday, 22nd April 1957. (J.J.Smith)

62. On the same day the up bay is occupied by the 6.20pm to Tonbridge. It is composed of two ex-LBSCR coaches and an ex-LCDR R class 0-4-4T, carrying BR no.31660. No passengers are visible on this peaceful Sunday afternoon. (N.Sprinks)

64. Waiting in the up bay on 15th August 1959 is H class 0-4-4T no.31319, ready to work a local service to Paddock Wood. One member of this class escaped the scrap merchants and can be found on the Bluebell Railway numbered 263. (A.E.Bennett)

65. Part of the goods shed is visible as class 4 2-6-4T no.80143 leaves the down bay on 16th June 1962 with the 5.21pm for Reading South. This train appeared in the public timetable as running to Tonbridge only. (S.C.Nash)

66. On the same day, another class 4 leaves for Tonbridge, but these coaches were empty. Rules would have once demanded that the van be at the back of a passenger train. The locomotive was built at Brighton in 1953, its companion (no.80064) surviving and now resident on the Bluebell Railway. (S.C.Nash)

67. Platform 1, the down bay, was often used for mail traffic. Beyond it is the yard's 15-ton crane. This replaced the two shown on the map, which were of 6 and 10 ton capacity. 2HAPs were introduced in 1957 and gradually replaced the wooden framed bodies of the type seen in picture no.50. (Lens of Sutton)

68. The east elevation was recorded on 19th March 1966, together with trolleybus overhead equipment. This system replaced the tramway (shown on the 1909 map) on 11th February 1930. (J.N.Faulkner)

69. No.56070 is heading the 06.30 stone train from Whatley Quarry (Somerset) to Allington sidings on 11th July 1988. The 2EPB unit forms the 13.53 Paddock Wood to Strood service. The goods yard closed on 3rd October 1977 and was subsequently occupied by Pickfords, as is evident. Sidings were also used by UKF for their fertiliser depot until 1991. (P.G.Barnes)

70. On 13th May 1979 the up bay (left) was taken out of use. This 1991 photograph shows that all three lines were signalled for up working. Platform 1 (down bay) became 3 and platform 3 became 1. The canopies were reduced in length in 1983. (P.G.Barnes)

Track diagram applicable from 13th May 1979. Reproduced from *Live Rail*, the journal of the Southern Electric Group. The sidings for stock berthing are no longer used regularly. In recent years the down bay and adjacent siding have been used exclusively by the engineers.

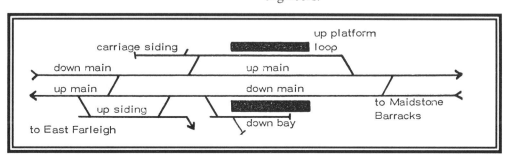

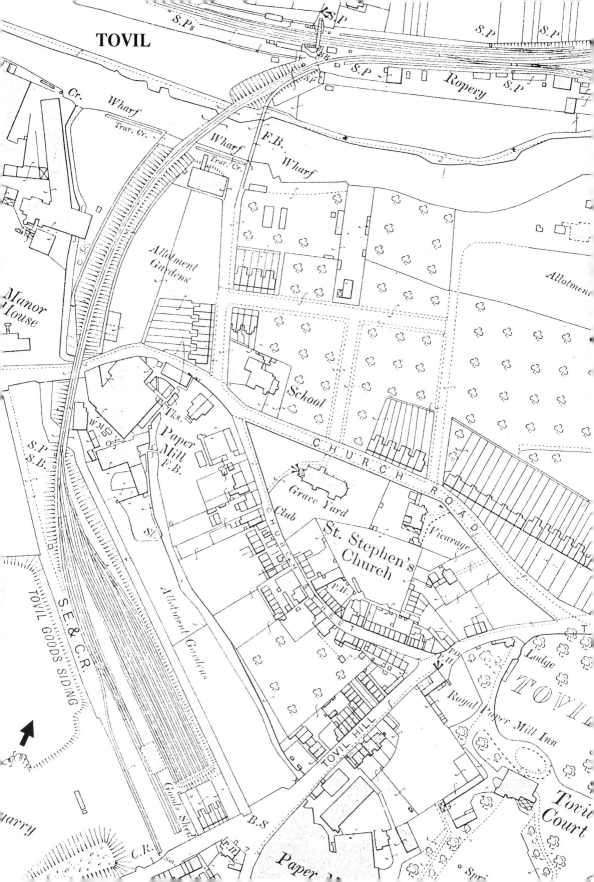

71. Tovil station served a residential area of Maidstone and was opened on 1st January 1884. Maidstone West goods yard is in the background. The station closed on 15th March 1943, but the footbridge was still in use 50 years later. (Lens of Sutton)

←———————

XX. The top right of this 1908 map overlaps the bottom left of the previous one. Tovil station is top centre and Tovil signal box is left of centre. The latter closed on 29th September 1929.

72. A 1979 view in the same direction as the previous picture (and from the footbridge therein) shows the curve to Tovil Goods, which had been closed on 3rd October 1977. The poles were erected in 1961 to carry wiring for electric locomotives working the sidings. They were fitted with pantographs and collector shoes, their classification being 71.
(M.J.Furnell)

73. The Tovil branch was intended to form part of the Loose Valley Line to Headcorn but it never became more than a goods siding. Seen in 1951, this massive lattice structure carried the line over the Medway and its commercial barges, the terminus being near the cloud of steam. (D.Cullum)

SOUTHERN RAILWAY.
This ticket is issued subject to the Company's
Bye-laws, Regulations and Conditions in their
Time Tables, Notices and Book of Regulations.
Beltring & Branbridges Halt to
Beltring & B.Halt   Beltring & B.Halt
Tovil   Tovil
TOViL
THIRD CLASS   THIRD CLASS
Fare 1/-   Fare 1/-
0537   0537

74.   Church Road and the paper mill are included in this study of the contractor's locomotive on the temporary bridge in 1883. The line carried raw materials to, and finished products from, a number of local paper mills. (Lens of Sutton)

75. Paper mills dominate this picture of Tovil Goods taken in November 1977, one month after its closure. There had been eleven parallel sidings at its zenith. Their opening is thought to have been 1886 but records are not complete. (M.J.Furnell)

EAST FARLEIGH

76. Many SER stations from the 1840s had staggered platforms, but few had a public highway between them. The 2.24pm from Paddock Wood on 13th August 1955 is about to be propelled over it towards Maidstone. (J.H.Aston)

XXI. The 1938 survey gives the full extent of the limited facilities. The nearby lock collapsed in 1909 and gave the railway a brief monopoly.

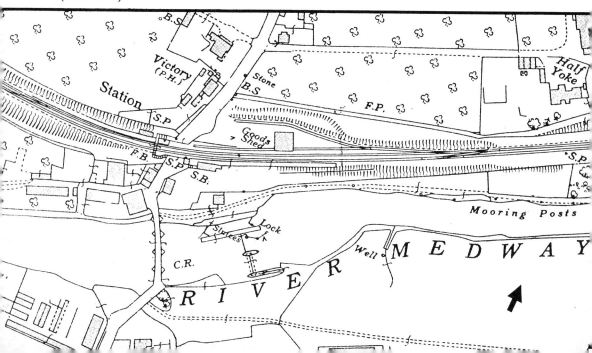

77. Bizarre handprints flank the headcode disc as class H no.31518 approaches the well stayed level crossing gate post. Notice also the platform extension and the weed covered track. (D.Cullum coll.)

78. The large goods shed was justified on account of the considerable fruit traffic handled from the many orchards surrounding the village. More commonly used on freight services, C class no.31716 leaves with the 11.02am to Maidstone West on 13th May 1961. (J.Low)

79.   Railway lanterns were often fashioned with great artistry and elegance, this compensating for their poor light output. Enjoy the fluted post with buttoned collars, the graceful taper of the lantern, the feminine curves of its supports, the tracery of its embellishments and the bulbous finial surmounting the multi-slotted ventilator. Only the lamp is missing. (A.E.Bennett)

80. This and the next picture were taken a few days before electric services commenced on 12th June 1961, hence the rusty conductor rail. The guard has his flag to hand as he waits for the photographer to complete his record of this dual braked C class and the bracketed lamp on the down side buildings. (J.Low)

81. The charm of the Medway Valley is evident as class H no.31308 arrives from Maidstone West with some retired main line coaches of Maunsell's design. The goods yard is fenced off, having closed on 3rd July 1961. The shed contained a small crane. (A.E.Bennett)

82. Soon after electric trains commenced, electric lighting was installed, but the signals remained oil lit. The SECR erected many concrete signal posts but this one is spalling badly. Between 1861 and 1921 the population of the village rose from 1500 to 1560, nothing to excite a railway traffic manager.
(British Rail)

83. The concrete post for the up starter was replaced by a metal tubular one of GWR style, whereas the signal opposite is mounted on a pair of redundant running rails, a standard SR practice after 1929. No.33205 is working the annual weed killing train on 21st June 1984.
(J.S.Petley)

84. No.6404 works the 16.23 Paddock Wood to Strood on 18th July 1988 and approaches the site of major engineering works adjacent to the river bank. The classical SER signal box appears well conserved. This and the hand-worked gates were still in use five years later.
(J.Scrace)

85. The lever handles were gleaming when photographed in December 1991, although most were out of use and painted white. Resignalling of the line had long been proposed. (P.G.Barnes)

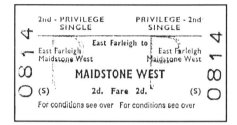

86. The relationship of the station (centre) to the lock (left) and the sluice (right) is shown well in this photograph from August 1991. The last commercial traffic on the Medway to Tonbridge was recorded in 1927. (J.Scrace)

Sec., G.S. Herbe, London. **SOUTH EASTERN, or LONDON & DOVER.** Sup. G. E. Ilbery.

Miles.	DOWN TRAINS.	1,2,& cheap a.m.	1 & 2 class. a.m.	1 2 3 class. a.m.	1 cl. exp. a.m.	1 & 2 mail. a.m.	1 2 3 class. p.m.	1 cl. exprs p.m.	1 & 2 class. p.m.	1 2 3 class p.m	1,2,3 Mail. p.m.	Sunday Trains. 1,2,& cheap a.m.	1 2 3 a.m.	1 & 2 a.m	1,2,3 p.m.	1 2 3 p.m.	1 & 2 Mail
	London Bridge	..	8 30	9 30	10 30	11 30	..	3 30	4 30	5 30	8 30	..	8 30	10 30	..	5 30	8 30
	Bricklayers' Arms ..	6 30	..	..	..	..	1 30	..	..	..	..	6 30	..	..	3 30	..	..
10¾	Croydon	6 57	8 53	9 57	..	11 55	1 57	..	4 53	5 57	9 4	6 57	8 57	10 53	3 57	5 57	9 4
19¾	Merstham	7 21	..	10 21	..	..	2 21	..	..	6 21	..	7 21	9 21	..	4 21	6 21	..
21	Reigate	7 26	9 18	10 26	..	12 19	2 26	..	5 18	6 26	9 32	7 26	9 26	11 18	4 26	6 26	9 32
26¼	Godstone	7 42	..	10 42	..	..	2 42	..	..	6 42	9 46	7 42	9 42	..	4 42	6 42	9 46
31¼	Edenbridge	7 55	..	10 55	..	..	2 55	..	5 38	6 55	10 0	7 55	9 55	..	4 55	6 55	10 0
36¼	Penshurst	8 10	..	11 10	..	..	3 10	..	..	7 10	10 13	8 10	10 10	..	5 10	7 10	10 13
41	**Tunbridge**	8 24	10 3	11 24	11 36	1 3	3 24	4 36	6 3	7 24	10 24	8 24	10 24	12 3	5 24	7 24	10 24
46	Tunbridge Wells....	8 45	10 23	11 45	11 52	1 25	3 45	4 52	6 23	7 45	..	8 45	10 45	12 23	5 45	7 45	..
46	Paddock Wood arrival	8 40	..	11 40	..	1 18	3 40	..	..	7 40	10 36	8 40	10 40	..	5 40	7 40	10 36
49	Yalding	8 48	..	11 48	..	..	3 48	..	..	7 48	..	8 48	10 48	..	5 48	7 48	..
51	Wateringbury	8 54	10 28	11 54	11 55	1 28	3 54	4 55	6 28	7 54	..	8 54	10 54	12 28	5 54	7 54	..
54	East Farleigh	9 3	..	12 3	..	..	4 3	..	..	8 3	..	9 3	11 3	..	6 3	8 3	..
56	Maidstone.... arrival	9 15	10 45	12 15	12 10	1 45	4 15	5 10	6 45	8 15	..	9 15	11 15	12 45	6 15	8 15	..
50½	Marden, depart from	9 53	..	12 53	..	..	3 53	..	..	7 53	..	8 53	10 53	..	5 53	7 53	..
53	Staplehurst	9 2	10 32	12 2	..	1 34	4 2	..	6 32	8 2	10 56	9 2	11 2	12 32	6 2	8 2	10 56
56	**Headcorn**	9 12	..	12 12	..	..	4 12	..	..	8 12	..	9 12	11 12	..	6 12	8 12	..
61¼	Pluckley	9 25	..	12 25	..	..	4 25	..	..	8 25	..	9 25	11 25	..	6 25	8 25	..
67	Ashford	9 39	11 2	12 39	12 18	2 4	4 39	5 18	7 2	8 39	11 27	9 39	11 39	1 2	6 39	8 39	11 27
76	Chilham............	10 5	..	1 5	12 38	..	5 5	5 38	..	9 5	..	10 5	12 5	..	7 5	9 5	..
82	Canterbury	10 18	11 37	1 18	12 50	2 40	5 18	5 50	7 37	9 18	..	10 18	12 18	1 37	7 18	9 18	..
93¼	Minster............	10 45	..	1 45	..	..	5 45	..	..	9 45	..	10 45	12 45	..	7 45	9 45	..
97½	Ramsgate..........	11 5	12 20	2 5	1 20	3 20	6 5	6 20	8 20	10 5	..	11 5	1 5	2 20	8 5	10 5	..
75	Westenhanger	10 3	11 23	1 3	..	2 24	5 3	..	7 23	9 3	..	10 3	12 3	1 23	7 3	9 3	..
82	Folkestone	10 20	11 39	1 20	12 43	2 40	5 20	5 43	7 39	9 20	12 0	10 20	12 20	1 39	7 20	9 20	12 0
88	**Dover**	10 45	12 0	1 45	1 0	3 0	5 45	6 0	8 0	9 45	12 15	10 45	12 45	2 0	7 45	9 45	12 15

OMNIBUSES will run to and from every Train at the London Bridge and Bricklayers' Arms Stations.—Fare, 6d., including 56 lbs weight of Luggage.

DAY TICKETS between all the Stations to go & return the same day, for one fare and a half. Day tickets issued on Saturdays, are returnable on Saturday, Sunday, or Monday; and Sunday tickets on Sunday or Monday.

FARES. FROM LONDON BRIDGE..	exps s. d.	1st cl s. d.	2d cl. s. d.	3d cl s. d.
Croydon........	..	2 0	1 6	0 11
Merstham	..	4 0	2 3	1 3
Reigate	..	4 4	2 6	1 4
Godstone	..	4 6	2 10	1 8
Edenbridge	..	5 0	3 4	2 0
Penshurst	..	5 10	3 8	2 3
Tunbridge	7 6	6 6	4 0	2 6
Tunbridge Wells	8 6	7 0	4 6	2 8
Paddock Wood..	..	7 0	4 6	2 8
Yalding	..	7 0	4 6	2 8

FARES. FROM LOND. BDGE	exps s. d.	1st cl s. d.	2d cl. s. d.	3d cl s. d.
Wateringbury ..	8 0	7 0	4 6	2 8
East Farleigh ..	..	7 0	4 6	2 8
Maidstone......	8 0	7 0	4 6	2 8
Marden	..	7 10	5 2	3 0
Staplehurst	..	8 6	5 8	3 4
Headcorn	..	9 0	6 2	3 8
Pluckley........	..	10 3	6 10	4 2
Ashford	13 6	11 6	7 4	4 8
Westenhanger ..	..	13 6	8 4	5 4
Folkestone......	18 0	15 0	10 0	6 0
DOVER........	18 0	15 0	10 0	6 0

WHITSTABLE BRANCH.

From Canterbury to Whitstable at 8 and 10 a.m., 12 noon, 2, 4, and 6 p.m. On SUNDAYS at 8½ and 11½ a.m., 2, 4, and 7 p.m.

From Whitstable to Canterbury at 8½ and 10½ a.m., 12½, 2½, 4½, and 6½ p.m. On SUNDAYS at 9½ a.m., 12½, 3½, 5½, and 8 p.m.

FARES, first class 1s.; second 6d.

Day Tickets, first class 1s. 6d.; second 10d.

A Courier's Carriage from the Bricklayers' Arms at 11 p.m., will be attached to the Goods train, at the special request of travellers desirous to reach Folkestone or Dover early in the morning. Fare 18s.—Children above One year, and under Ten years, will be charged Half-price.

Eng. in Chief, R. Stephenson. **SOUTH EASTERN, or LONDON & DOVER.** Res. Eng. P. W. Barlow.

Miles.	Up Trains.	1, 2,3 Mail a.m.	1 2 3 clss. a.m.	1 cl. exp. p m.	1 & 2 class a.m.	1,2,3 Mail a.m.	1 & 2 class. a.m.	1.2.3. class. p.m.	1 cls. exprs p.m.	1& 2 clss p.m	12& chp. p.m		Sunday Trains. 1,2ml a.m.	1.2,3 a.m.	1,2,3 a.m.	1 & 2 a.m	1,2,3 p.m.	1.2.& chp.	
0	**Dover**	1 30	6 0	8 0	8 15	9 0	11 15	1 0	3 15	4 15	5 0	..	1 30	6 0	8 0	10 0	3 0	5 0	..
5¾	Folkestone...........	1 45	6 14	8 10	8 27	9 14	11 27	1 14	3 25	4 27	5 14	..	1 45	6 14	8 14	10 12	3 14	5 14	..
12¼	Westenhanger..........	..	6 35	..	8 44	9 35	11 44	1 35	..	4 44	5 35	..	..	9 35	8 35	10 29	3 35	5 35	..
51¼	Ramsgate	..	5 35	7 40	7 55	8 35	10 55	12 35	2 55	3 55	4 35	..	..	5 35	7 35	9 40	2 35	4 35	..
47	Minster	..	5 45	..	..	8 45	..	12 45	..	..	4 45	..	..	5 45	7 45	..	2 45	4 45	..
35¾	Canterbury............	..	6 11	8 4	8 25	2 11	11 25	1 11	3 19	4 25	5 11	..	..	6 11	8 11	10 10	3 11	5 11	..
29¾	Chilham	..	6 27	8 15	..	9 27	..	1 27	3 30	..	5 27	..	..	6 27	8 27	..	3 27	5 27	..
20¾	Ashford	2 22	6 54	8 35	9 1	9 54	12 1	1 54	3 50	5 1	5 54	..	2 22	6 54	8 54	10 46	3 54	5 54	..
26	Pluckley	..	7 10	..	..	10 10	..	2 10	..	..	6 10	..	..	7 10	9 10	..	4 10	6 10	..
31¼	**Headcorn**..........	..	7 23	..	..	10 23	..	2 23	..	..	6 23	..	..	7 23	9 23	..	4 23	6 23	..
34¼	Staplehurst	2 54	7 31	..	9 31	10 31	12 31	2 31	..	5 31	6 31	..	2 54	7 31	9 31	11 16	4 31	6 31	..
37	Marden	..	7 40	..	..	10 40	..	2 40	..	..	6 40	..	..	7 40	9 40	..	4 40	6 40	..
51¾	Maidstone	..	7 15	8 45	9 20	10 15	12 20	2 15	4 0	5 20	6 15	..	..	7 15	9 15	11 5	4 15	6 15	..
50	East Farleigh..........	..	7 20	..	..	10 20	..	2 20	..	..	6 20	..	..	7 20	9 20	..	4 20	6 20	..
47	Wateringbury	..	7 28	8 54	9 30	10 28	12 30	2 28	4 9	5 30	6 28	..	..	7 28	9 28	11 15	4 28	6 28	..
45½	Yalding	..	6 35	..	..	10 35	..	2 35	..	..	6 35	..	..	7 35	9 35	..	4 35	6 35	..
41¾	Paddock Wood	..	7 52	..	..	10 52	..	2 52	..	..	6 52	..	..	7 52	9 52	..	4 52	6 52	..
51¾	Tunbridge Wells........	..	7 50	9 2	9 42	10 50	12 42	2 50	4 17	5 42	6 50	..	..	7 50	9 50	11 27	4 50	6 50	..
46¾	**Tunbridge**..........	3 24	8 6	9 15	9 57	11 6	12 57	3 6	4 30	5 57	7 6	..	3 24	8 6	10 6	11 42	5 6	7 6	..
51	Penshurst	..	8 24	..	..	11 24	..	3 24	..	..	7 24	..	..	8 24	10 24	..	5 24	7 24	..
56	Edenbridge............	..	8 38	..	10 22	11 38	..	3 38	..	..	7 38	..	..	8 38	10 38	..	5 38	7 39	..
61	Godstone..............	..	8 52	..	..	11 52	..	3 52	..	..	7 52	..	..	8 52	10 52	..	5 52	7 52	..
66½	Reigate	4 9	9 8	..	10 48	12 8	1 47	4 8	..	6 47	8 8	..	4 9	9 10	11 8	12 32	6 8	8 8	..
67¾	Merstham	..	9 14	..	..	12 14	..	4 14	..	..	8 14	..	..	9 15	11 14	..	6 14	8 14	..
76¾	Croydon	4 30	9 37	..	11 11	12 37	2 11	4 37	..	7 11	8 37	..	4 30	9 37	11 37	12 56	6 37	8 37	..
87	Bricklayers' Arms......	..	..	..	..	..	..	5 15	..	..	9 15	..	..	..	12 15	..	..	9 15	..
88	**London Bridge** ...	5 0	10 0	10 30	11 45	1 15	2 45	..	5 45	7 45	..	..	5 0	10 15	..	1 30	7 15	..	..

FARES. FROM DOVER TO	exp. s. d.	1 cls. s. d.	2 cls. s. d.	3 cls. s. d.
Folkstone..............	1 6	1 0	0 9	0 6
Westenhanger..........	..	2 8	1 8	0 10
Ramsgate	8 0	7 0	5 0	4 0
Ashford	5 0	4 0	2 9	1 9
Pluckley..............	..	5 6	3 3	1 10
Headcorn	..	6 6	4 0	2 4
Staplehurst	..	7 3	4 4	2 8
Marden	..	7 8	4 6	8 0

FARES. FROM DOVER TO	exp. s. d.	1 cls. s. d.	2 cls. s. d.	3 cls. s. d.
Maidstone..............	12 0	10 0	6 0	3 8
East Farleigh	....	9 6	5 6	3 6
Wateringbury	11 6	9 6	5 6	3 6
Yalding	....	9 0	5 4	3 4
Paddock Wood..........	....	8 8	5 3	3 4
Tunbridge Wells........	13 0	10 6	6 4	3 9
Tunbridge..............	12 0	9 8	5 10	3 6
Penshurst	....	10 6	6 4	3 9

FARES. FROM DOVER TO	exprs. s. d.	1 cls. s. d.	2 cls. s. d.	3cl. s. d.
Edenbridge	....	11 6	7 0	4 0
Godstone	....	12 6	7 10	4 4
Reigate	....	13 6	8 8	4 8
Merstham	....	13 6	8 8	4 10
Croydon................	....	14 0	9 6	5 6
Bricklayers' Arms	18 0	15 0	10 0	6 0
LONDON BRIDGE	18 0	15 0	10 0	6 0

Manager, J. Y. Akerman. **SOUTH EASTERN.—Greenwich Branch.—Length of Line 3¾ Miles.**

The trains run each way every ¼ of an hour from 8 a.m. till 10 p.m.; on Sundays from 8 till ¼ to 11, and from ¼ past 1 till 10.

FARES.—1st class 8d.; 2nd class 6d.; 3rd class 4d.; and if with return ticket, 1st class 1s. 2nd class 10d.

ANNUAL TICKETS may be had on the following terms, by all the trains:—first class, £7 10s.—second class, £5 2s. from the 1st May until the 31st December.

An extra train leaves London at a ¼ past 10 p.m. calling at all the stations.

Timetables for 1st May 1846.

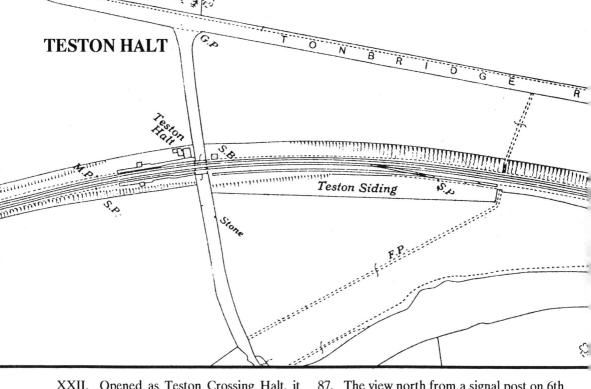

TESTON HALT

XXII. Opened as Teston Crossing Halt, it became Teston halt, as shown on this 1938 map. The siding was not then listed for public use, although it predates the halt.

87. The view north from a signal post on 6th September 1952 reveals that the platforms were only suitable for a two-coach push-pull formation. The waterside meadows make this an appealing part of the journey. (D.Cullum)

88. Looking towards Paddock Wood in September 1952 we see the site of the former siding (left) and the tiny signal box. This controlled lifting barriers from 7th September 1977 and was dispensed with when they were worked under CCTV from March 1978. (Pamlin Prints)

89. Cars line up on the road from West Farleigh as class H no.31266 accelerates towards Yalding on 31st August 1958. A van was often added at that time of year for seasonal fruit traffic. The halt closed on 2nd November 1959. (P.Hay)

WATERINGBURY

90. An 1886 view includes the top hatted stationmaster, the station's only signal post and a canopy on the up platform with stanchions dangerously near to its edge. All the buildings were still standing in 1993. (Lens of Sutton)

XXIII. The 1908 survey marks a crane (Cr.) in the yard. It was of 4-ton capacity. The station building is on the right.

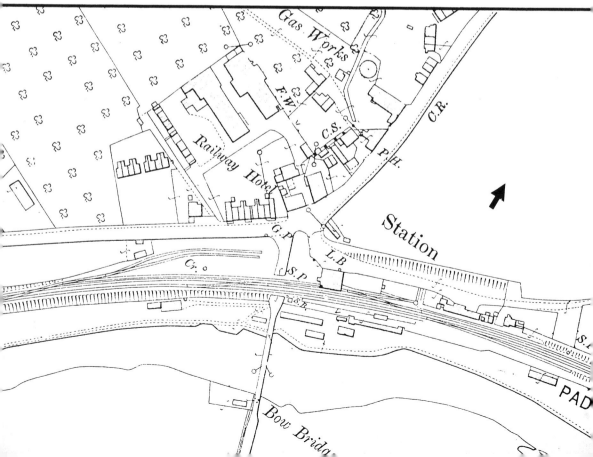

91. This was the only station south of Maidstone to be of this elaborate style. It could not have impressed the local population, as this diminished over the 60 years to 1920 from 1400 to 1200. (Lens of Sutton)

92. A solitary passenger on the up platform meditates upon the tranquil river on 6th June 1952. A new shelter and signal box had appeared since photo 90 was taken. A goods line, for which an independent pair of gates was provided (as at Hampton), ran across the road, quite an unusual occurrence. (D.Cullum)

93. The goods shed and the crane are seen clearly as we leave southwards on 9th August 1952. Only two privies spoil the view of Bow Bridge and the boats. The river was now an asset to the railway, rather than a competitor. (H.C.Casserley)

94. As prosperity was increasing during the 1950s, more Londoners were able to afford a day in the country and ramblers excursions became popular. The 9.56am from Victoria on 2nd May 1954 was far too long for the platform. The empty coaches are now leaving for Maidstone West behind class U1 no. 31902. (N.Sprinks)

95. The 4.22pm Maidstone West to Sevenoaks on 6th May 1961 was worked by C class no. 31244, devoid of a headcode. The rain had probably deterred the fireman from moving it from the tender. (J.H.Aston)

96. Goods engines were not uncommon on passenger duties in the final years. Seen on 13th May 1961, class C no. 31716 waits to depart with the 1.24 to Maidstone West while class Q1 0-6-0 arrives with the 1.26 departure for Tonbridge, also minus a headcode. (J.Low)

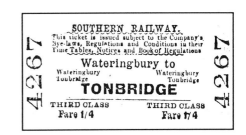

SOUTHERN RAILWAY.
This ticket is issued subject to the Company's Bye-laws, Regulations and Conditions in their Time Tables, Notices and Book of Regulations

Wateringbury to

Wateringbury
Tonbridge

Wateringbury
Tonbridge

TONBRIDGE

THIRD CLASS
Fare 1/4

THIRD CLASS
Fare 1/4

98. Seen in 1988, the footbridge was erected prior to the 1961 electrification, eliminating the foot crossing between the staggered platforms. The SR's concrete lamppost had been replaced. (J.Scrace)

97. On 10th June 1961, class H no. 31305 heads a southbound train. The goods shed and the yard closed on 4th September of that year, the ground signal still being in position. The following week many of the firemen would be without a job. (A.E.Bennett)

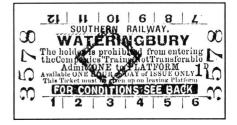

SOUTHERN RAILWAY.
WATERINGBURY
The holder is prohibited from entering the Company's Trains not Transferable
Admit ONE to PLATFORM
Available ONE HOUR of DAY of ISSUE ONLY
This Ticket must be given up on leaving Platform
FOR CONDITIONS SEE BACK
1 | 2 | 3 | 4 | 5 | 6

YALDING

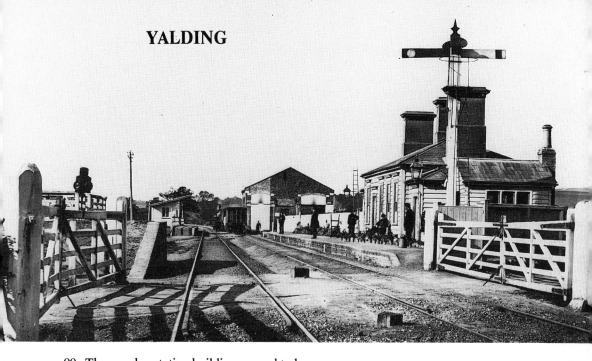

99. The wooden station building proved to be a false economy as it burnt down in 1893. It is seen here in 1870, along with the simple signalling system, the control box being to the right of the post. (Lens of Sutton)

XXIV. The line from Maidstone is on the right of this 1908 edition.

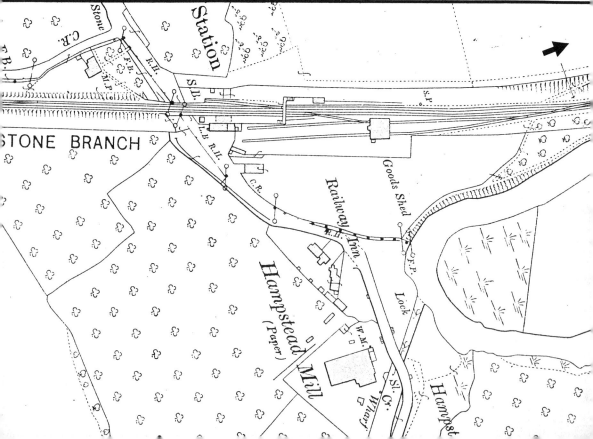

100. Unlike the other goods sheds on the route, two tracks passed through this one. It contained a crane rated at 25 cwt. The track on the left was infilled to allow road vehicles to enter. (D.Cullum)

101. A northward view in 1958 shows that platform lengthening had reduced the staggering of the platforms. The footbridge had been erected prior to 1895. The goods yard closed on 27th May 1963. (H.C.Casserley coll.)

Yalding (P., 2,314). Gracious little township, nestling amid orchards in heart of Kent's "hopland," with unusually long old recessed bridge spanning two streams, and oasthouses and attractive old-world thatched dwellings rising above green-verged street. E.E. and later church (16th-c. brasses, 15th-c. monument); 17th-c. moated Vicarage. Angling (free). Important soap and hopwash manufactory near station.

1938 RAC Gazetteer

102. Running tender first with the late 3.28pm from Tonbridge on 6th May 1961 is class C no. 31244. Two coaches would have presented no problem to the footplate crew but coal dust flying from the tender might have done. The only remedy was large quantities of water. (J.H.Aston)

103. Seen on the same day, class H no. 31177 waits to leave with the 3.22pm from Maidstone West. The gates were opened by hand. The 27-lever signal box was closed on 22nd June 1986 when the level crossing became an automatic open crossing. Half barriers were provided in December 1992. (J.H.Aston)

S. E. & C. R. (SEE BACK)
Available Day of issue ONLY.
Yalding to
MAIDSTONE WEST
Revised Fare   Revised Fare
2/0½ First Class 2/0½
Maidstone West   Maidstone West

006   006

104. A 1967 photograph shows a camping coach in the disconnected dock siding. The starting signal with colour light distant was changed to a 3-aspect colour light on 29th October 1972. Below the signal, bushes largely obscure the siding to Plant Protection Ltd. which was in use from about 1950 to 31st December 1970. (J.N.Faulkner)

105. With a yellow end and a warning triangle, unit no. 6065 passes the up platform as it runs in from Paddock Wood. Little remains of the dock siding and nothing of the Pullman car that once graced the site. (J.Scrace)

106. The 1894 building was similar to that provided at Halling in the same decade. For the first 70 years of the line the population of the village remained steady at about 2500. The building was extant in 1993, although the windows had been bricked up. (J.Scrace)

107. The evening sun casts shadows as class H 0-4-4T no. 31551 passes over the Medway, the route doing so for the last time. The river turns west here to Tonbridge. (J.J.Smith)

2nd - SINGLE   SINGLE - 2nd

Yalding to

Yalding

Yalding

Beltring and-

Beltring and

Branbridges Halt

Branbridges Halt

BELTRING & BRANBRIDGES HALT

(S)   8d. Fare 8d.   (S)

For conditions see over   For conditions see over

3526

SOUTHERN RAILWAY.

This ticket is issued subject to the Company's Bye-laws, Regulations and Conditions in their Time Tables, Notices and Book of Regulations.

Beltring & Branbridges Halt to

Beltring & B.Halt   Beltring & B.Halt

Tovil   Tovil

TOVIL

THIRD CLASS   THIRD CLASS

Fare 1/-   Fare 1/-

0538

SOUTHERN RAILWAY.

Issued subject to the bye-laws, Regulations & Conditions in the Company's Bills and Notices.

H.M.P. on LEAVE.

Yalding to

Yalding   Maidstone West

MAIDSTONE WEST

THIRD CLASS   THIRD CLASS

NOT TRANSFERABLE.

1674

2nd - CHEAP   CHEAP - 2nd

OFF PEAK   OFF PEAK

Earls Court   Beltring

(5227A) to   to   (5227A)

BELTRING   **EARLS COURT**

via LTR & London (SR)   via London (SR) & LTR

(S)   (S)

For conditions see over   For conditions see over

0047

BELTRING

108. Class C 0-6-0 no. 31716 runs over the level crossing on 6th May 1961 with the 2.22pm from Maidstone West. In the distance are the points of a public siding which was closed on 5th June 1961. (J.H.Aston)

109. The coal man has used his skill to fill the bunker of class H no. 31177 on 6th June 1961. It is working the 2.00pm Sevenoaks to Maidstone West with a set of BR coaches, a type rarely seen on the line. (J.H.Aston)

110. The signal box became a gate box on 5th September 1961 and automatic half barriers were in use from 20th October 1982. The installation is seen on 18th July 1988. North of Beltring, a trailing siding from the down line entered the civil engineer's tip. (J.Scrace)

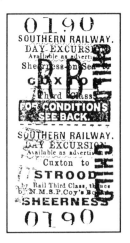

111. Electro-diesel no. 73105 has its retractable shoes down on the conductor rail as it hums over the level crossing with an engineers train on 1st August 1990. (J.S.Petley)

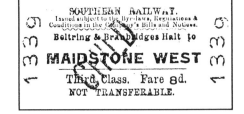

PADDOCK WOOD

112.   Until the line to Maidstone opened, the station was named "Maidstone Road" and passengers transferred to road transport. The far sighted directors of the SER laid out the station with two through lines for fast trains. The Maidstone line bears left beyond the building. "A" box (left) closed on 26th June 1932. (Lens of Sutton)

113.   A closer view of the up end reveals a wagon turntable by the cattle dock (left). Nearby is a horse box, probably detached from a recent down train. The up side buildings and footbridge date from 1893. (Lens of Sutton)

114. Having rounded the 17-chain curve in the background on 13th August 1960, an H class propels a Maidstone West to Tonbridge service into the up platform. The driving coach was converted from a Maunsell corridor vehicle. The signal box closed on 1st April 1962. (J.N.Faulkner)

115. Crowds leave the 12.16pm Tonbridge to Maidstone West service on 27th May 1961, passengers no longer having the benefit of a roof on the footbridge. However, the crew has the benefit of a tender cab while running class Q1 no.33037 in reverse. (J.Scrace)

116. This and the next photograph were taken on 3rd June 1961. Although partial electric services commenced that month, they ran to the steam timetable, owing to a shortage of the new stock. Here class H no.1308 waits with a Maidstone West to Tonbridge service. (A.E.Bennett)

117. Wagons reached the goods shed (right background) from the wagon turntable seen in picture no.113. General freight facilities ceased on 3rd January 1960. Class C no.31588 arrives with a train for Maidstone West. The local population doubled in the twenty years to 1971 to nearly 5000. (A.E.Bennett)

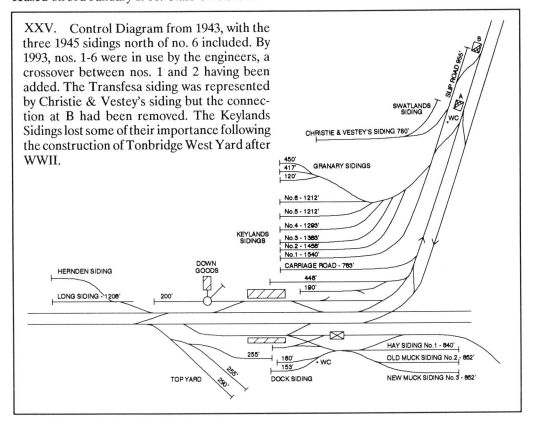

XXV. Control Diagram from 1943, with the three 1945 sidings north of no. 6 included. By 1993, nos. 1-6 were in use by the engineers, a crossover between nos. 1 and 2 having been added. The Transfesa siding was represented by Christie & Vestey's siding but the connection at B had been removed. The Keylands Sidings lost some of their importance following the construction of Tonbridge West Yard after WWII.

SLIP ROAD 955'

B

SWATLANDS SIDING

A

WC

CHRISTIE & VESTEY'S SIDING 780'

450'
417'   GRANARY SIDINGS
120'

No.6 - 1212'

No.5 - 1212'

No.4 - 1293'

KEYLANDS   No.3 - 1363'
SIDINGS   No.2 - 1456'
                No.1 - 1540'

CARRIAGE ROAD - 783'

HERNDEN SIDING   DOWN
                        GOODS   446'

                                        190'

LONG SIDING - 1206'   200'

                                                        HAY SIDING No.1 - 840'

                                        255'   OLD MUCK SIDING No.2 - 852'
                                        160'
                            255'   153'   WC

TOP YARD   290'   DOCK SIDING   NEW MUCK SIDING No.3 - 852'

118. On the left is the depot of TRANSFESA (**Trans**portes **Fe**rroviario's Especiales **SA**), importers of Spanish agricultural produce by rail. It contains three sidings and was officially opened on 28th October 1974. The 12.46 from Strood is entering the bay platform on 21st October 1988. (J.Scrace)

119. The 11.16 Hoo Junction to Tonbridge benefits from reversible running through platform 2, the connection to the up line at the down end having been removed. The electro-diesel is no.73108 and the date is 3rd November 1988. (J.Scrace)

120.   The 09.53 to Strood waits in the remaining bay platform on 7th December 1991. The up bay was used by Hawkhurst trains until they ceased to run on 12th June 1961. With the cessation of through running from Maidstone to London, the station has become a junction once more. (J.Scrace)

Maps and other views of Paddock Wood can be found in our *Branch Line to Hawkhurst* **and** *Redhill to Ashford* **albums.**

MP Middleton Press

Easebourne Lane, Midhurst. West Sussex. GU29 9AZ
Tel: (0730) 813169   Fax: (0730) 812601

Write or telephone for our latest booklist

BRANCH LINES

BRANCH LINES TO MIDHURST
BRANCH LINES AROUND MIDHURST
BRANCH LINES TO HORSHAM
BRANCH LINE TO SELSEY
BRANCH LINES TO EAST GRINSTEAD
BRANCH LINES TO ALTON
BRANCH LINE TO TENTERDEN
BRANCH LINES TO NEWPORT
BRANCH LINES TO TUNBRIDGE WELLS
BRANCH LINE TO SWANAGE
BRANCH LINES TO LONGMOOR
BRANCH LINE TO LYME REGIS
BRANCH LINE TO FAIRFORD
BRANCH LINE TO ALLHALLOWS
BRANCH LINES AROUND ASCOT
BRANCH LINES AROUND WEYMOUTH
BRANCH LINE TO HAWKHURST
BRANCH LINES AROUND EFFINGHAM JN
BRANCH LINE TO MINEHEAD
BRANCH LINE TO SHREWSBURY
BRANCH LINES AROUND HUNTINGDON
BRANCH LINES TO SEATON AND SIDMOUTH
BRANCH LINES AROUND WIMBORNE
BRANCH LINES TO EXMOUTH
BRANCH LINE TO LYNTON
BRANCH LINE TO SOUTHWOLD

SOUTH COAST RAILWAYS

BRIGHTON TO WORTHING
CHICHESTER TO PORTSMOUTH
BRIGHTON TO EASTBOURNE
RYDE TO VENTNOR
EASTBOURNE TO HASTINGS
HASTINGS TO ASHFORD
SOUTHAMPTON TO BOURNEMOUTH
ASHFORD TO DOVER
BOURNEMOUTH TO WEYMOUTH
DOVER TO RAMSGATE

COUNTRY RAILWAY ROUTES

BOURNEMOUTH TO EVERCREECH JN
READING TO GUILDFORD
WOKING TO ALTON
BATH TO EVERCREECH JUNCTION
GUILDFORD TO REDHILL
EAST KENT LIGHT RAILWAY
FAREHAM TO SALISBURY
BURNHAM TO EVERCREECH JUNCTION
REDHILL TO ASHFORD
YEOVIL TO DORCHESTER
ANDOVER TO SOUTHAMPTON

SOUTHERN MAIN LINES

HAYWARDS HEATH TO SEAFORD
EPSOM TO HORSHAM
CRAWLEY TO LITTLEHAMPTON
THREE BRIDGES TO BRIGHTON
WATERLOO TO WOKING
VICTORIA TO EAST CROYDON
EAST CROYDON TO THREE BRIDGES
WOKING TO SOUTHAMPTON
WATERLOO TO WINDSOR
LONDON BRIDGE TO EAST CROYDON
BASINGSTOKE TO SALISBURY
SITTINGBOURNE TO RAMSGATE
YEOVIL TO EXETER
CHARING CROSS TO ORPINGTON
VICTORIA TO BROMLEY SOUTH
ORPINGTON TO TONBRIDGE
FAVERSHAM TO DOVER
SALISBURY TO YEOVIL

LONDON SUBURBAN RAILWAYS

CHARING CROSS TO DARTFORD
HOLBORN VIADUCT TO LEWISHAM
KINGSTON & HOUNSLOW LOOPS
CRYSTAL PALACE AND CATFORD LOOP
LEWISHAM TO DARTFORD
MITCHAM JUNCTION LINES
WEST CROYDON TO EPSOM

STEAMING THROUGH

STEAMING THROUGH EAST HANTS
STEAMING THROUGH SURREY
STEAMING THROUGH WEST SUSSEX
STEAMING THROUGH THE ISLE OF WIGHT
STEAMING THROUGH WEST HANTS

OTHER BOOKS

GARRAWAY FATHER & SON
LONDON CHATHAM & DOVER RAILWAY
INDUSTRIAL RAILWAYS OF THE S. EAST
WEST SUSSEX RAILWAYS IN THE 1980s
SOUTH EASTERN RAILWAY
TILLINGBOURNE BUS STORY
MILITARY DEFENCE OF WEST SUSSEX
BATTLE OVER PORTSMOUTH
BATTLE OVER SUSSEX 1940
SURREY WATERWAYS
KENT AND EAST SUSSEX WATERWAYS
HAMPSHIRE WATERWAYS
LEIGH PARK
BRIGHTON'S TRAMWAYS
EAST GRINSTEAD THEN & NOW